CRAZY BOOKS

Funny Insults

with Glen Singleton

Crazy Book of Insults
First published in 2003 by Hinkler Books Pty Ltd
17–23 Redwood Drive
Dingley VIC 3172 Australia
www.hinklerbooks.com

Reprinted 2003

ISBN: 1865156892

Cover designer: Peter Tovey Studios
Editor: Rose Inserra
Typesetting: Midland Typesetters
Printed and bound in Australia

Crazy Book of Insults

You are so dumb you planted birdseed because you wanted to raise canaries.

You are so dumb you gave cough syrup to your pony because someone told you it was a little horse.

You are so dumb you fed money to your cow because you wanted to get rich milk.

You are so dumb you wore a wet shirt all day because the label said 'wash and wear'.

You are so dumb you ate yeast and shoe polish for breakfast because you wanted to rise and shine in the morning.

You are so dumb you run around and around your bed so you can catch up with your sleep.

You are so dumb you got fired from your job as an elevator operator because you couldn't remember the route.

You are so dumb you think a cartoon is something you sing in the car.

You are so dumb you tripped over a cordless phone.

You are so dumb you burnt your ear because you were ironing when the phone rang.

You are so dumb you burnt your other ear when the caller rang back.

You are so dumb, when you tried to make a birthday cake the candles melted in the oven.

You are so dumb you take your bicycle to bed because you don't want to walk in your sleep.

Janet: 'What's the difference between a cake and a school bus?'

Jill: 'I don't know.'

Janet: 'I'm glad I didn't send you to pick up my birthday cake!'

You are so dumb you think a buttress is a female goat!

You are so dumb you threw away your guitar because it had a hole in it.

You are so dumb you told your teacher you couldn't write an essay on goldfish because you didn't have any waterproof ink.

You are so dumb you got fired from the banana factory for throwing out all the bent ones.

My gym teacher is so dumb he runs around the exam rooms hoping to jog students' memories.

You are so dumb you think Hamlet is an omelette with bacon.

'Our teacher talks to herself in class, does yours?'

'Yes, but she doesn't realize it. She thinks we're listening!'

Student: 'I don't think I deserve a zero on this test.'

Teacher: 'No, neither do I but it was the lowest I could give you!'

You are so dumb you think software is a floppy hat.

Ben's teacher thinks Ben is a wonder child.

She wonders whether he'll ever learn anything.

Teacher: 'That's the stupidest boy in the whole school.'

Mother: 'That's my son.'

Teacher: 'Oh! I'm so sorry.'

Mother: 'You're sorry?'

'How old would you say I am, Francis?' the teacher asked.

'Forty,' said the boy promptly.

'What makes you think I'm forty?' asked the puzzled teacher.

'My big brother is twenty,' he replied, 'and you're twice as silly as he is!'

You are so dumb you saw a moose's head hanging on a wall and went into the next room to find the rest of it!

You are so dumb you kept banging your head against the wall because it felt so good when you stopped.

You are so dumb you went round and round in a revolving door looking for the doorknob.

You are so dumb you think a polygon is a dead parrot.

You are so dumb you invented a parachute that opens on left-handed screwdriver.

You are so dumb you invented a one-way escalator.

You are so dumb you could be brainwashed with an eyedropper.

You are so dumb you invented a chocolate teapot.

You are so dumb you invented waterproof teabags.

You are so dumb you invented a parachute that opens on impact.

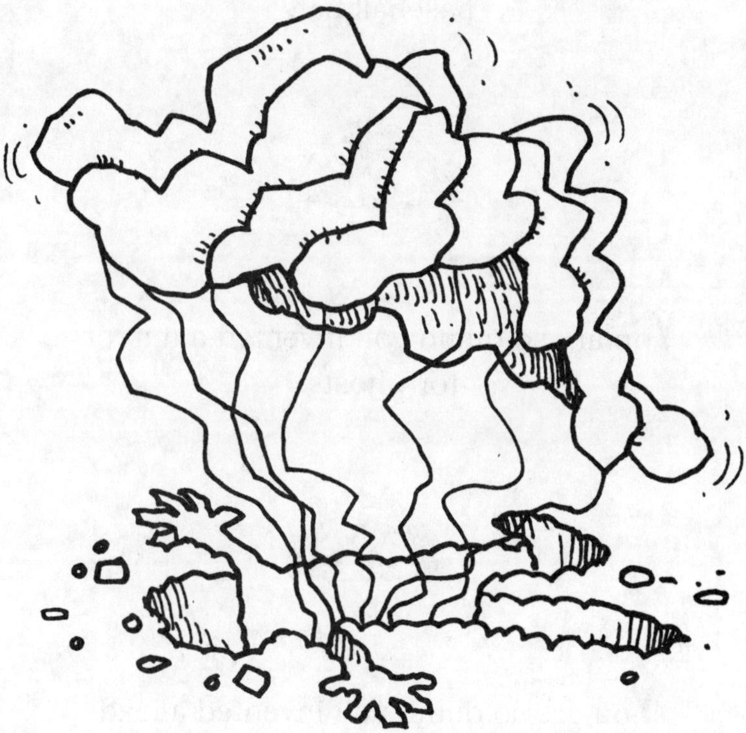

You are so dumb you invented a fly screen on a submarine.

You are so dumb you invented a glass baseball bat.

You are so dumb you invented a mirror for ghosts.

You are so dumb you invented a lead balloon.

You are so dumb you invented a solar-powered torch.

You are so dumb you invented an ashtray for a motorbike.

You are so dumb you invented black windows.

You are so dumb you invented rubber nails.

You are so dumb you invented an ejector seat on a helicopter.

You are so dumb you invented non-stick glue.

You are so dumb you invented sugar cube fishing bait.

You are so dumb you invented a bikini for Eskimos.

You are so dumb you invented underwear for kilt wearers.

You are so dumb you ate a worm when you were asked to do a bird impression.

You are so dumb you turned away from Disneyland after seeing a sign that read 'Disneyland Left'.

You are so dumb you got fired from the M&M factory for throwing away all the W's.

You are so dumb you climbed over a glass wall to see what was on the other side.

You are so dumb you think that a kilo of feathers weighs less than a kilo of lead.

You are so dumb you got your money back after having your mind read.

You are so dumb you called your pet zebra 'Spot'.

Boy: 'They say ignorance is bliss.'

Girl: 'Then you should be the happiest boy in the world!'

Everyone calls you 'Fog' because you are dense and wet.

You are so dumb you take a pencil to bed to draw the curtains.

Boy: 'I'll tell you everything I know.'

Girl: 'In that case you'll be speechless!'

You are so dumb you write letters to your grandpa slowly because he can't read very fast.

You are so dumb you jump up and down before taking medicine because the label reads 'Shake well before using'.

Dick and Jane were arguing over the breakfast table.

'Oh, you're so stupid!' shouted Dick.

'Dick!' said their father. 'That's quite enough! Now say you're sorry.'

'Okay,' said Dick. 'Jane, I'm sorry you're stupid.'

You are so dumb your computer has whiteout all over the screen.

You are so dumb, you saw a sign outside a police station that read 'Man Wanted for Robbery', and went in and applied for the job!

You are so dumb you think a fjord is a Scandinavian motor car.

You are so dumb, when you went hitchhiking you got up early so there wouldn't be much traffic around.

You are so dumb, when I asked you what the weather was like, you replied, 'It's too foggy to tell.'

You are so dumb, when the lifesaver told you not to jump in the pool because there was no water, you replied, 'It's alright, I can't swim.'

You are so dumb, when you bought a train ticket and the ticket seller asked, 'Where to?' you replied, 'Back here of course!'

You are so dumb, when you held up the music store you told them to give you the lute.

You are so dumb, when you went shoplifting you stole a free sample.

You are so dumb you fell out of a tree after you were told to rake up the leaves.

You are so dumb, when you tried to do some glass blowing you inhaled and got a pane in the tummy.

You are so dumb, when you flew a helicopter you turned the propeller off because you couldn't stand the draft.

You are so dumb, when your Greek mythology teacher asked you to name something that was half-man and half-beast, you replied, 'Buffalo Bill'.

You are so dumb, when I told you that your shoes had to be soled, you sold them.

You are so dumb, when you went shoplifting you hurt your back trying to lift the corner store.

You are so dumb, when you dress up as a pirate you put a patch over both eyes.

You are so dumb, if you ever have a brain transplant, the brain will be sure to reject you.

Your dad is so dumb, when he locked his keys in the car he called a mechanic to get the family out.

You are so dumb you slept under your car because you wanted to wake up oily in the morning.

You are so dumb you spent two hours in a department store looking for a cap with a peak at the back.

You are so dumb, when you went skiing you skied up the slope and caught the chair lift down.

You are so dumb at Halloween you carve a face on an apple and go bobbing for pumpkins.

You are so dumb you have a stop sign at the top of your ladder.

You are so dumb, when you went water-skiing you spent your whole holiday looking for a sloping lake.

Your uncle, Farmer Peter is so dumb he packed up and moved to the city when he heard that the country was at war.

You are so dumb you got seventeen of your friends to accompany you to the movies because you heard it was not for under-18s.

You are so dumb you left your job as a telephonist because you kept hearing voices.

You are so dumb you took a gun with you when you went white-water rafting, so you could shoot the rapids.

You are so dumb you fell in the sink while tap dancing.

You are so dumb you threw away your doughnut because it had a hole in the middle.

Your dad is so dumb he walked into the electricity company with a $20 note in each ear because he received a bill saying he was $40 in arrears.

Your dad is so dumb he only gets a half-hour lunch break because if he took any longer he would have to be re-trained.

Our goalkeeper is so dumb he won't catch the ball because he thinks that's what the net is for.

How many toes does an idiot have?

Take off your socks and count them.

You are so dumb you forgot your twin brother's birthday.

Don't let your mind wander — it's too little to be let out alone.

You are so dumb you put stamps on the faxes that you send.

With you here, your village must be missing its idiot.

You would be out of your
depth in a puddle.

You are not as stupid as you look.
That would be impossible.

I'd leave you with one thought if you
had somewhere to put it.

You are so dumb it takes you an hour to
cook one-minute noodles.

You are so dumb you think the English Channel is a British TV station.

You are so dumb you took your mobile phone back to the shop because it came without a cord.

If someone offered you a penny for your thoughts, they'd expect some change.

You are so dumb you leapt from a window to try out your new jump suit.

You should go to a dentist and have some wisdom teeth put in.

You have an open mind. Ideas just slip straight out.

You are so dumb you stared at the orange juice container because it said 'Concentrate'.

You are so dumb it takes you three hours to watch 'Sixty Minutes'.

Your dad is so dumb he took a ruler to bed to see how long he slept.

Your dad is so dumb he sold his car for gas money.

You are so dumb you can't pass a blood test.

Your brother is so dumb, when he swam across the English Channel he got tired half way and swam back.

You are so dumb you put a chicken in a hot bath so it would lay hard-boiled eggs.

Your mum is so dumb she put lipstick on her forehead because she wanted to make up her mind.

You are so dumb you asked for a price check at the $2 shop.

Your mum is so dumb, when you asked her to buy you a colour TV she asked, 'What colour?'

Your dad is so dumb he locked himself in a motorbike.

Your granddad is so dumb he got locked in a supermarket overnight and died of starvation.

Your grandma is so dumb, when the sign said 'Don't Walk' she froze and got hit by a bus.

You are so dumb you order a cheeseburger without cheese.

Your mum is so dumb, when she fills in forms that say 'Sign Here', she writes 'Taurus'.

You are so dumb you threw the butter out of window because you wanted to see a butterfly.

You are so dumb you tried to drown a fish.

You are a few clowns short of a circus.

You are a few fries short
of a Happy Meal.

You are an experiment
in artificial stupidity.

You are a few beers short of a six-pack.

You are a few peas short of a casserole.

You are one Fruit Loop
shy of a full bowl.

You are as smart as bait.

You are so dumb you wear two
sets of pants when you play golf
in case you get a hole in one.

Your elevator doesn't go all
the way to the top floor.

You forgot to pay your brain bill.

Your sewing machine is out of thread.

Your antenna isn't picking up all the channels.

'I've changed my mind.'

'Great, does the new one work any better?'

How do you make a stupid person laugh on a Thursday?

Tell him a joke on Monday.

'How dare you tell everyone I'm stupid.'

'Sorry, I didn't realise it was a secret.'

How can you kill a dumb person with a coin?

Throw it under an oncoming truck.

You are so dumb you put your pet cat next to the computer to keep an eye on the mouse.

'**D**o you find me entertaining?'

'You're too dim to entertain a thought.'

I hear you were the last one born in your family. I can understand that. You're enough to discourage anyone.

You are so dumb you put a coin in a parking meter and waited for a gumball to come out.

You are so dumb, when you missed the 44 bus you took the 22 twice instead.

You are so dumb you ordered your sushi well done.

You are so dumb you invented a solar powered flashlight.

You are so dumb you got hit by a parked car.

You are so dumb you thought Sherlock Holmes was a housing project.

You are so dumb you bought a horse because you wanted to play water polo.

You are so dumb you called the 24-hour supermarket to see when they closed.

You are so dumb, when you heard 90% of all accidents occur around the home you moved.

I like you a lot. But then, I've never had good taste.

You are so dumb you bought a video camera to record cable TV shows at home.

Calling you stupid would be an insult to stupid people.

Go ahead, tell us everything you know. It'll only take 10 seconds.

You are a monument to the human race. And you know what pigeons do to monuments.

He has a mind like a steel trap – always closed!

He is living proof that man can live without a brain!

He is the kind of a man that you would use as a blueprint to build an idiot.

He's not stupid; he's possessed by a retarded ghost.

You are so dumb you went to night school to learn to read in the dark.

I bet your brain feels as good as new, seeing that you've never used it.

I don't know what makes you so stupid, but it really works!

I don't think you are a fool. But then what's my opinion against thousands of others?

I heard you went to have your head examined but the doctors found nothing there.

I know you are nobody's fool but maybe someone will adopt you.

You are so dumb you tiptoe past the medicine cabinet so that you don't wake the sleeping pills.

I would ask you how old you are but I know you can't count that high.

I'd like to leave you with one thought . . . but I'm not sure you have anywhere to put it!

If I ever need a brain transplant, I'd choose yours because I'd want a brain that had never been used.

You're so unpopular even your answering machine hangs up on you.

If what you don't know can't hurt you you'll live forever.

If you stand close enough to him you can hear the ocean.

If your brain was chocolate it wouldn't fill an M&M.

Keep talking, someday you'll say something intelligent.

You are so dumb you refused to buy a ticket for the door prize because you already have a door.

So a thought crossed your mind? Must have been a long and lonely journey.

There is no vaccine against stupidity.

Just because you have a sharp tongue does not mean you have a keen mind.

Are you always this stupid or are you making a special effort today?

Brains aren't everything. In fact in your case they're nothing.

You have a photographic mind. It's a pity it has never been developed.

You look lost in your thoughts — unfamiliar territory for you.

You don't know the meaning of the word 'fear', but then again you don't know the meaning of most words.

You are so dumb you tried to fit a cake into a typewriter so you could write 'Happy Birthday'.

You are the kind of friend a person can depend on. You're always around when you need me.

You do the work of three men:
Larry, Curly & Moe.

You are so dumb you threw a rock at
the ground, and missed.

You are so dumb if you had a brain
you'd take it out and play with it.

You're a miracle of nature. You have an IQ of 2 and you're still able to speak.

If you were any dumber you'd have to be watered twice a week.

You're so dumb you can't even spell the word 'dumb'.

You are so dumb you couldn't pour water out of a boot if the instructions were written on the bottom of the heel.

You are so dumb you put your socks on inside out because there was a hole on the outside.

I'll try being nicer if you try being smarter.

The closest you'll ever come to a brain storm is a light drizzle.

You are so dumb you couldn't find your butt if both your hands were tied behind your back.

It's perfectly all right to have an unexpressed thought. In fact, in your case I recommend it.

I would never enter into a battle of wits with an unarmed person.

You are so dumb you think martial arts are paintings by the sheriff.

You obviously fell out of the Stupid Tree and hit every branch on the way down.

You know I do understand you. I seem to have a way with dumb animals.

You are so dumb you think people who live in Paris are called parasites.

People say you're a perfect idiot. I tell them you may not be perfect but you are doing a great job being an idiot.

You are so dumb you think birds that are kept in captivity are called jail birds.

You are so dumb you push when playing tug of war.

You are so dumb, when you call your dog you put two fingers in your mouth and shout 'Rover'.

Boy: 'You've got a face like a million dollars.'

Girl: 'Have I really?'

Boy: 'Sure, it's green and wrinkly!'

Handsome Harry: 'Every time I walk past a girl, she sighs.'

Wisecracking William: 'With relief!'

Everyone has the right to be ugly, but you abused the privilege.

Bill: 'My sister has lovely long hair, all down her back.'

Will: 'Pity it's not on her head!'

Woman: 'When I'm old and ugly, will you still love me?'

Man: 'I do, don't I?'

What's small, annoying and really ugly?

I don't know but it comes when I call my sister's name.

'My sister went on a crash diet.'

'Is that why she looks a wreck?'

Every time I take my girlfriend out for a meal, she eats her head off.

She looks better that way.

You are so ugly, when you went on a package tour near where headhunters live you were the only survivor.

Turn the other cheek. On second thoughts, don't. The view is just as ugly on that side.

You are so ugly, when you enter a room the mice jump on chairs.

You are dark and handsome. When it's dark you are handsome.

Last time I saw someone as ugly as you I had to pay admission.

You are so ugly the only dates you get are on a calendar.

You are so ugly you have to trick or treat over the phone.

Doctor, Doctor, I have a hoarse throat.

The resemblance doesn't end there.

Your mum is so ugly she went to a beauty salon and it took three hours . . . for an estimate.

Your sister is so ugly the garbageman won't even pick her up.

'Haven't I seen you on TV?'

'Well yes, I do appear off and on. How do you like me?'

'Off.'

Don't look out of the window. People will think that it's Halloween.

'Do you think that I'll lose my looks when I get older?'

'With luck, yes.'

'My husband always carries my photo in his pocket. It once saved his life when a mugger tried to stab him.'

'Your face would stop anything.'

Doctor, Doctor, I'm so ugly what can I do about it?

Hire yourself out for Halloween parties.

Every time you open your mouth your foot falls out.

'I've just come back from the beauty salon.'

'What a pity it was closed.'

I'm not saying my wife isn't good looking but when she goes to the doctor he tells her to open her mouth and go 'Moooo'.

'What would it take to make me look good?'

'A lot of distance between you and me.'

'Boys fall in love with me at first sight.'

'I bet they change their minds when they look again.'

'Shall I put the TV on?'

'Well it would certainly improve the view in here.'

You are so ugly, when you joined an ugly contest they said, 'Sorry, no professionals allowed.'

You are so ugly, when you were born your mother said, 'What a treasure!' and you father said, 'Yes, let's go bury it.'

You are so ugly they push your face into dough to make cookies.

You are so ugly even Rice Bubbles won't talk to you!

'Daddy, Daddy, there's a monster at the door with a really ugly face.'

'Tell him you've already got one!'

You are so ugly people go as you to Halloween parties.

You are so ugly the government moved Halloween to your birthday.

You are so ugly they didn't give you a costume when you auditioned for Star Wars.

You are so ugly, when you try to take a bath the water jumps out!

You are so ugly, when you walk into a bank they turn off the surveillance cameras.

You are so ugly you could turn Medusa to stone!

You are so ugly you won the prize for best costume at the Halloween Party even though you were just picking up your sister.

You are so ugly you made an onion cry.

You are so ugly your mum had to tie a steak around your neck to get the dog to play with you.

You are so ugly your mum had to get drunk to breast feed you.

You mum is so ugly I heard that your dad first met her at the pound.

You mum is so ugly on Halloween the kids trick or treat her by phone!

Your mum is so ugly they pay her to put her clothes on in strip joints.

You mum is so ugly your father takes her to work with him so that he doesn't have to kiss her goodbye.

If I were as ugly as you I'd wear a mask.

You're so ugly, when a wasp stings you it has to shut its eyes!

Don't you need a licence to be that ugly?

You are so ugly, when you were a baby your mum had to feed you with a slingshot.

You are so ugly, when you stand on the beach the tide won't come in.

You are so ugly, when you were born the doctor turned you over and said, 'Look. Twins.'

Your face is so ugly it would make a train take a dirt road.

Either you're very ugly or your neck has stepped in something.

Your sister has everything a man desires — bulging muscles and moustache.

Your sister is so ugly she was asked to remove her mask at a masked ball — and she wasn't wearing one.

Your feet are so smelly your shoes refuse to come out of the closet.

You might not know much but you lead the league in nostril hair.

Teacher: 'Billy, stop making ugly faces at the other students!'

Billy: 'Why?'

Teacher: 'Well, when I was your age, I was told that if I kept making ugly faces, my face would stay that way.'

Billy: 'Well, I can see you didn't listen.'

'I've kept my youthful complexion.'

'So I see, all spotty.'

'Why are you bathing in such dirty water?'

'It wasn't dirty when I got in.'

'You smell funny.'

'That's my soap. I don't suppose you've smelt it before.'

'Is that a new perfume I smell?'

'It is, and you do.'

What's the difference between you and a wild camel? One is a big, smelly, bad tempered beast and the other is an animal.

I've heard you're the big noise around here. I think you should cut back on the baked beans.

You don't need to use an insult, you could just use your breath.

First Boy: 'Do you keep yourself clean?'

Second Boy: 'Oh, yes, I take a bath every month, whether I need one or not!'

Your breath is so bad that people look forward to your farts.

Your mum is so fat a picture of her fell off the wall!

Your mum is so fat all the restaurants in town have signs that say: 'Maximum Occupancy: 200 Patrons OR Your Mum'.

Your mum is so fat at a restaurant when they give her the menu she replies, 'Yes please.'

Your mum is so fat Bill Gates couldn't afford to pay for her liposuction.

Your mum is so fat Dr Martens needed three cows just to make her a pair of shoes.

Your mum is so fat every time she puts an apple in her mouth people try to roast her.

Your mum is so fat her belly jiggle is the first ever perpetual motion machine.

Your mum is so fat her belt is the size of the equator.

Your mum is so fat her cereal bowl came with a lifeguard.

Your mum is so fat her clothes have stretch marks.

Your mum is so fat her high school year book picture was an aerial picture.

Your mum is so fat her picture takes two frames.

Your mum is so fat I had to take a train and two buses just to get on her good side.

Your mum is so fat instead of wide leg jeans, she wears wide load.

Your mum is so fat she can lie down and stand up and her height doesn't change.

Your mum is so fat she had her baby pictures taken by satellite.

Your mum is so fat she had her ears pierced by harpoon.

Your mum is so fat she has her own area code.

Your mum is so fat she has more chins than the Chinese phone book.

Your mum is so fat she has to buy two airline tickets.

Your mum is so fat she has two stomachs . . . one for meats and one for vegetables.

Your mum is so fat she makes Big Bird look like a rubber duck.

Your mum is so fat she makes
Free Willy look like a tic tac.

Your mum is so fat she makes sumo
wrestlers look anorexic.

Your mum is so fat she needs a hula
hoop to keep up her socks.

Your mum is so fat she needs a
watch on both arms because she
covers two time zones.

Your mum is so fat she sets off car alarms when she runs.

Your mum is so fat she was born with a silver shovel in her mouth.

Your mum is so fat she shows up on radar.

Your mum is so fat she went on a seafood diet . . . whenever she saw food she ate it.

Your mum is so fat she went to the movies and sat next to everyone.

Your mum is so fat she's got smaller fat women orbiting around her.

Your mum is so fat she's on both sides of your family.

Your mum is so fat she's like the Bermuda Triangle; when kids run around her they get lost.

Your mum is so fat the horse on her Polo shirt is real.

Your mum is so fat the last time she saw 90210 was on the scale.

Your mum is so fat they had to grease the bathtub to get her out.

Your mum is so fat they tie a rope around her shoulders and drag her through a tunnel when they want to clean it.

Your mum is so fat, when her beeper went off they thought she was backing up.

Your mum is so fat, when I tried to drive around her I ran out of gas.

Your mum is so fat, when she bends over we lose an hour of daylight.

Your mum is so fat, when she bungee jumps she brings down the bridge too.

Your mum is so fat, when she goes to a restaurant she doesn't get a menu she gets a quote.

Your mum is so fat, when she goes to an all you can eat buffet they have to install speed bumps.

Your mum is so fat, when she gets in an elevator it has to go down.

Your mum is so fat, when she goes to the circus she sees the big top and asks, 'Where can I try that on?'

Your mum is so fat, when she leaves the beach everybody shouts, 'The coast is clear.'

Your mum is so fat, when she runs she makes the CD player skip . . . at the radio station.

Your mum is so fat, when she sits on the beach Greenpeace shows up and tries to tow her back into the ocean.

Your mum is so fat, when she steps on the scale it says, 'One at a time please.'

Your mum is so fat, when she steps on the scale it says, 'Sorry we don't do livestock.'

Your mum is so fat, when she tiptoes everyone yells, 'Stampede!'

Your mum is so fat, when she turns around they throw her a welcome back party.

Your mum is so fat, when she walked in front of the TV I missed three commercials.

Your mum is so fat, when she was diagnosed with the flesh eating disease the doctor gave her five years to live.

Your mum is so fat, when she went to get a water bed they put a blanket across the Pacific Ocean.

Your mum is so fat, when she went to the beach she's the only one who got a tan.

Your mum is so fat, when the police showed her a picture of her feet she couldn't identify them.

Your mum is so fat your bathtub has stretch marks.

Your mum is so fat she climbed Mt Everest with one step.

Your mum is so fat, when she fell in love she broke it.

There's nothing wrong with you
that death wouldn't cure.

Go and sit down. Nobody can stand you.

'You'd make a good exchange student.'

'Do you think so?'

'Yes we might be able to exchange you
for someone nice.'

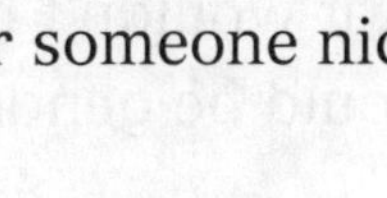

'You remind me of a camel.'

'Why?'

'You give me the hump.'

If we were to kill everybody who hates you, it wouldn't be murder; it would be genocide!

I'm not being rude, you're just insignificant.

You were so annoying on the airline flight that the steward told you to go and play outside.

Doctor, Doctor, everyone hates me.

Don't be stupid, not everyone has met you yet.

Waiter, do you serve crabs in this restaurant?

Yes sir, we serve anyone.

You are so lazy you got a job in a bakery to have a good loaf.

He's good at everything he does. And as far as I can see he usually does nothing.

You're so lazy, that if you woke up with nothing to do, you'd go to bed with it only half done.

'Mum, there's a man at the door collecting for the Old Folks' Home,' said the little boy.

'Shall I give him Grandma?'

Jane: 'Do you like me?'

Wayne: 'As girls go, you're fine and the sooner you go, the better!'

A girl walked into a pet shop and said, 'I'd like a frog for my brother.'

'Sorry,' said the shopkeeper. 'We don't do exchanges!'

First Man: 'My girlfriend eats like a bird.'

Second Man: 'You mean she hardly eats a thing?'

First Man: 'No, she eats slugs and worms.'

'Do you think, Professor, that my girlfriend should take up the piano as a career?'

'No, I think she should put down the lid as a favour!'

'My brother's been practising the violin for ten years.'

'Is he any good?'

'No, it was nine years before he found out he wasn't supposed to blow!'

James: 'I call my girlfriend Peach.'

John: 'Because she's soft, and beautiful as a peach?'

James: 'No, because she's got a heart of stone.'

When Wally Witherspoon proposed to his girlfriend, she said, 'I love the simple things in life, Wally, but I don't want one of them for a husband!'

Maria: 'Whatever will Tammy do when she leaves school? She's not smart enough to get a job!'

Leonie: 'She could always be a ventriloquist's dummy.'

My girlfriend talks so much that when she goes on vacation she has to spread suntan lotion on her tongue!

Jane: 'Do you ever do any gardening?'

Wayne: 'Not often. Why?'

Jane: 'You look as if you could do with some remedial weeding.'

'Can I go swimming now, Mum?' asked the child.

'No – there are sharks at this beach,' said his mother.

'Dad's swimming!'

'Yes, he's got a million dollars' life insurance.'

A woman woke her husband in the middle of the night.

'There's a burglar in the kitchen eating the cake I made this morning!' she said.

'Who should I call?' asked her husband. 'The police or an ambulance?'

My big brother is such an idiot. The other day I saw him hitting himself over the head with a hammer. He was trying to make his head swell, so his hat wouldn't fall over his eyes!

A man walks into a bar with a skunk under his arm.

Barman: 'You can't bring that smelly thing in here.'

Skunk: 'Sorry. I'll leave him outside.'

Person 1: 'I've never been so insulted in all my life.'

Person 2: 'You haven't been trying.'

'Waiter, I'd like burnt steak and soggy chips with a grimy, bitter salad.'

'I'm afraid the chef won't cook that for you, sir.'

'He did yesterday.'

'Mummy, Mummy, Dad has been run over by a steamroller.'

'Shut up and slide him under the door.'

'Mummy, Mummy, Daddy's on fire.'

'Hurry up and get the marshmallows.'

'Mummy, Mummy, why do I keep going round in circles?'

'Shut up or I'll nail your other foot to the floor.'

'Mummy, Mummy, are you sure you bake bread this way.'

'Shut up and get back in. I can't close the oven door.'

'Mummy, Mummy, Dad's going out.'

'Shut up and throw some more petrol on him.'

'Mummy, Mummy, Daddy's hammering on the roof again.'

'Shut up and drive a bit faster.'

'Mummy, Mummy, why is Dad running in zig zags?'

'Shut up and keep shooting.'

'Mum, why do I have to go to school? The kids all make fun of me and all the teachers hate me.'

'Because you're the headmaster, son.'

'Mummy, Mummy, why are we pushing the car off the cliff?'

'Shut up or you'll wake your father.'

What do you call a guy who hangs around musicians?

A drummer.

'This piece of music is haunting.'

'That's because you're murdering it.'

'What shall I sing next?'

'Do you know Bridge Over Troubled Waters*?'*

'Yes.'

'Then go and jump off it.'

You are such a bad typist you type sixty mistakes a minute.

You are so careless, when you tried to fit a new window you broke it with a hammer.

You are so tight with your money you sit at the back of the bus to get a longer ride for your money.

'The girl who sits beside me in maths is very clever,' said Alec to his mother. 'She's got enough brains for two.'

'Perhaps you'd better think of marriage,' said his mum.

You are such a bad cook even the maggots get take-away.

Your family is so poor, when the doorbell rings your sister has to shout out, 'Ding, Dong.'

You are so slow you can't even catch your breath.

As an outsider, what do you think of the human race?

The cost of living is so high.

So why do you bother living?

Here's 50 cents. Call all your friends and bring me back the change.

Your dog is so slow he brings in last week's newspaper.

Is it true your brother is an only child?

Instead of drinking from the fountain of knowledge, you just gargled.

You are so forgetful you wrote a letter to yourself and forgot to sign it. When it arrived, you didn't know who sent it.

Someone told me you are not fit to live with pigs but I stuck up for you and said you were.

If it's true that opposites attract, you'll meet someone who is good-looking, intelligent and cultured.

They say that truth is stranger than fiction. And you are the proof.

I'll never forget the first time we met – although I keep trying.

You are growing on me – like a wart.

You are so boring you won't even talk to yourself.

Your family is so poor, when I went inside your house I accidentally stepped on a cockroach and your whole family came out singing, 'Clap your hands, stomp your feet, thank the Lord that we got meat!'

You are so poor, when I went to your house and asked where the bathroom was you said, 'Third bottle to the left.'

Father: 'I want to take my girl out of this terrible maths class.'

Teacher: 'But she's top of the class!'

Father: 'That's why it must be a terrible class!'

'Hey teacher, the class isn't really that dull . . . just you.'

'Hey teacher, I'd love to stick it out through the rest of class but I have a life.'

'Hey teacher, I'd be a foul person too if I had to look at us all day.'

'Hey teacher, that last lesson you gave us was wonderful. Just one question. What were you talking about?'

'Hey teacher, I'd hate to be grossly underpaid for my work. Does it bother you?'

You are lower than the fluff in an earthworm's belly button.

Your granddad is so old he can whistle
and clean his teeth at the same time.

I am going to get a fur for you.
As fur as possible.

'What smells worse than a bad egg?'

'You do!'

Teacher: 'Why didn't you answer me, Stuart?'

Stuart: 'I did, I shook my head.'

Teacher: 'You don't expect me to hear it rattling from here, do you?'

'Can you cure my fleas?'

'Maybe, what's wrong with them?'

'Do you like my cottage pie?'

'Umm, next time try taking the drains out first.'

'This food isn't fit for a pig.'

'I'll get some for you that is then.'

My sister has such a sharp tongue we don't need a knife to carve the Sunday roast.

'I think a lot of people will go to his funeral.'

'Yes, to really make sure he is dead.'

'He has an answer for everything.'

'Yes, the wrong one.'

'He's a boon to the whole area.'

'More like a baboon.'

First teacher: 'What's wrong with young Jimmy today? I saw him running around the playground, screaming and pulling at his hair.'

Second teacher: 'Don't worry. He's just lost his marbles.'

'People like that don't grow on trees you know.'

'No, they normally swing under them.'

'Did you hear that he was buried face down?'

'Why?'

'So he could see where he was going.'

His death won't be listed under 'Obituaries', more like 'Neighbourhood Improvements'.

'I hear she is a business woman.'

'Yes, her nose is always in other people's business.'

They call him 'Caterpillar' because he has got where he is by crawling.

They call him 'Rope' because he is always stringing people along.

He is always very courteous. He apologises after he has hit you.

'Coach, how would you have played that last shot?'

'In disguise.'

'What position do you play in the football team?'

'I'm not sure, though the coach calls me one of the drawbacks.'

Jack: 'Mum, all the boys at school call me Big Head.'

Mum: 'Never mind, dear, just run down to the grocery store and collect the big bag of apples I ordered in your cap.'

'I hear the team's prospects are looking up.'

'I didn't know you were leaving.'

Our new player is called 'Cinderella' because he keeps running away from the ball.

They call the boxer Picasso because he spends most of the time on the canvas.

'**C**oach, how do I stand for a team trial?'

'You don't stand, you grovel.'

'I've never played so badly.'

'You mean you've actually played before?'

'I love golf. I could play like this forever.'

'Don't you want to improve?'

'Dad, I think you're getting taller'.

'What makes you think that?'

'Well, lately I've noticed that your head is sticking through your hair.'

'My doctor says I should give up football.'

'So he's seen you play too then.'

'How many people work in your office?'

'About half of them.'

She'll lose her looks when she gets older, which just proves how lucky she is.

'**M**y boyfriend whispers that he loves me.'

'Well it's not the sort of thing that he'd admit out loud.'

'**W**henever I go to the store, they shake my hand.'

'I expect it's to make sure you don't put it in the till.'

'You'll just have to give me credit.'

'Well I certainly won't be giving you cash.'

'I do lots of exercise.'

'I thought so. That's why you're so long-winded.'

'Why have you given me this long piece of rope?'

'Well they say that if you give someone enough rope they'll hang themselves.'

You remind me of a calendar. Your days are numbered.

You are like an oil well. Always boring.

You remind me of a toenail. The sooner you get cut down to size the better.

'Do you know what nice people do at the weekend?'

'No.'

'I didn't think you would.'

Mary: 'Do you think my sister's pretty?'

Gary: 'Well, let's just say if you pulled her pigtail, she'd probably say, "Oink, oink!"'

'**I** love biscuits.'

'That's because you're crackers.'

'**H**ow long can someone live without a brain?'

'How old are you?'

You are so dumb you planted coins in your garden because you wanted to raise some hard cash.

'I don't like soup.'

'I expect you can't get it to stay on the fork can you?'

You're multi talented. You do a hundred things badly.

'Whisper those three little words that would make my day.'

'Get a life!'

I can't understand why people say my girlfriend's legs look like matchsticks.

They do look like sticks – but they certainly don't match!

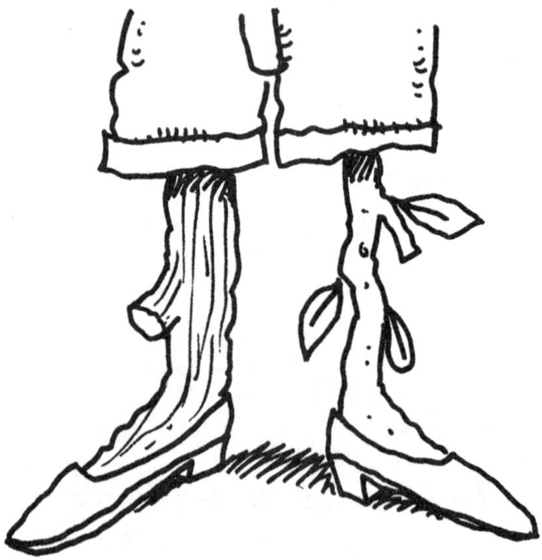

'I've been asked to get married hundreds of times.'

'Yes, but your parents don't count.'

'If we get married do you think you'll be able to live on my income?'

'Yes, but what will you live on?'

You can always spot my boyfriend at a party. Look for two people talking, if one looks bored, then the other is my boyfriend.

He spent a thousand dollars getting his bad breath cured then found out that no-one liked him anyway.

'I love looking in the mirror admiring my looks. Do you think that's vanity?'

'No, just a vivid imagination.'

'Do you notice how my voice fills the hall?'

'Yes, and did you notice how many people left to make way for it?'

'I can play piano by ear.'

'And I can fiddle with my toes.'

My cousin spent heaps on deodorant, until he found out people just didn't like him.

'How do you find my breath?'

'Offensive, it's keeping you alive.'

'We should try and fight air pollution.'

'You could start by stopping breathing.'

You dad is so hairy they filmed 'Gorillas in the Mist' in his shower.

That's a nice outfit you're wearing. Do you always wear seconds?

Any similarity between you and a human is purely coincidental!

Anyone who told you to be yourself couldn't have given you worse advice.

You don't bore people with long speeches. You can bore them with a short speech.

Did your parents ever ask you to run away from home?

Boy: 'I want to work badly.'

Girl: 'You usually do.'

Do you ever wonder what life would be like if you'd had enough oxygen at birth?

Do you want people to accept you as you are or do you want them to like you?

Don't you have a terribly empty
feeling – in your skull?

Do you still love nature,
despite what it did to you?

Hi, I'm a human being! What are you?

How did you get here? Did someone
leave your cage open?

He's such a loser his bride turned up with a date on their wedding day.

I bet your mother has a loud bark!

You are so scared you wear a lifejacket when you sleep on a water bed.

I could make a monkey out of you, but why should I take all the credit?

I don't consider you a vulture. I consider you something a vulture would eat.

I hear the only place you're ever invited to go is outside.

I hear you were born on a farm. Any more in the litter?

I thought of you all day today. I was at the zoo.

I'd like to help you out. Which way did you come in?

I'd love to go out with you, but my favorite commercial is on TV.

I haven't spoken to my sister for over a year. I don't like to interrupt her.

I'm busy now. Can I ignore you some other time?

First Girl: 'Whenever I'm down in the dumps, I buy myself a new hat.'

Second Girl: 'Oh, so that's where you get them!'

You shoot your mouth off so much you must brush your teeth with gunpowder.

He loves his wife so much, not only did he put in a swimming pool, he even bought a shark to go in it.

Pardon me, but you've obviously mistaken me for someone who cares.

Some day you will find yourself – and wish you hadn't.

Some women are blonde on their mother's side, some from their father's side – your mum is from Peroxide.

If your mum has one more facelift she'll have a beard.

Is that your face or did
your neck throw up?

Boy: 'I just got this puppy
for my brother.'

Girl: 'That was good value as a swap!'

You are so slow you have
to speed up to stop!

Your teeth are so yellow that your eyes
light up when you close your mouth.

You are as sharp as a bowling ball.

You will never be the man your mother is.

When I look into your eyes, I can see cows grazing.

Your dad is so hairy, Bigfoot takes pictures of him.

You should treat me with a little more respect. Someday it's going to be my tax dollars paying for your prison cell!

You're so skinny, you could hang glide on a corn chip.

I don't know what your problem is, but I bet there's no cure.

Hold still, I'm trying to imagine you with a personality.

Mother: 'Cathy, get your little sister's hat out of that puddle!'

Cathy: 'I can't, Mum. She's got it strapped too tight under her chin.'

Hi, I'm Earth. Have we met?

You're so old you fart dust.

You are no longer beneath my contempt.

Are you just visiting this planet?

May a thousand fleas from a camel's back infest your armpit and keep you warm at night.

I would have done the same thing
for someone I liked.

'I got a gold watch for my girlfriend.'

'I wish I could make a trade like that!'

How do you keep a nerd in
suspense for 24 hours?

I'll tell you tomorrow.

I'm not saying you're a pinhead but how many angels can dance on your head?

Your incompetence is an inspiration to morons everywhere.

When you and your mum had an argument, it was a battle of the Wits – Nit versus Dim. When your dad joined in, it was Nit versus Dim verses Half.

If I had a brother like you, I'd put myself up for adoption.

You remind me of drugs, a slow working dope.

You are proof that even God makes mistakes sometimes.

When God was handing out brains you must have been holding the door.

You're a legend in your own mind!

When you were born the doctor slapped your mother.

When I want your opinion I'll rattle your cage.

When they made you they broke the mold. Then, they found the moldmaker, dragged him out into the street and beat him up.

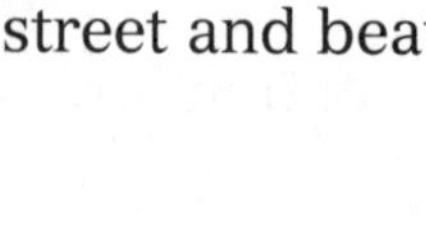

'My girlfriend says that if I don't give up golf, she'll leave me.'

'Say, that's tough, old man.'

'Yeah, I'm going to miss her . . .'

Your house is so nasty I tripped over a rat and a cockroach stole my wallet.

You remind me of the southern most portion of a northern bound horse.

If I throw a stick, will you go away?

That isn't your forehead, it's your hair trying to run away from your face.

Did your parents meet on a Petri dish?

Mary: 'I've a soft spot for you.'

Harry: 'Ah, really?'

Mary: 'Yes – in the middle of a bog!'

You are so short and hairy, when you walk around the house your mother screams, 'Mouse!'

You are so skinny you could do push ups under a door.

I'd wring your neck if I could find it.

What are you going to do for a face when the monkey wants his butt back?

When you were born your mother did not know which end to put the nappy on.

You have such a striking face. So tell me, how many times were you struck?

You have the face of a saint. A Saint Bernard, that is.

When you were born your mother was charged for littering.

You are so dense light bends around you.

You're not acting like yourself lately. I noticed the improvement immediately.

'Mrs Johnston, your daughter would be a fine dancer, except for two things.'

'What are they?'

'Both feet!'

My dad is so mean with money he heats the knives so we don't use too much butter.

My dad is so mean with money he told us that Santa was too old to get around anymore.

My dad is so mean with money he told us that when the ice cream van plays music it has run out of ice cream.

'That dress fits you like a glove. It sticks out in five places.'

One day Joe's mother said to his father, 'It's such a nice day, I think I'll take Joe to the zoo.'

'I wouldn't bother,' said his father. 'If they want him, let them come and get him!'

You have such bad handwriting you ought to become a doctor.

You are the type of boy that your mother doesn't want you to hang around with.

I wouldn't say you were hard-hearted but if I kicked you in the heart I'd break my foot.

Uncle Hubert noticed that his nephew, Johnny was watching him the whole time. 'Why are you always looking at me?' he asked.

'I was just wondering when you were going to do your trick,' replied Johnny.

'What trick?' asked Uncle Hubert.

'Well, Mum says you drink like a fish.'

Roger was in a full bus when a fat lady opposite said to him, 'If you were a gentleman, you'd stand up and let someone else sit down.'

'And if you were a lady,' Roger replied, 'you'd stand up and let four people sit down!'